DUE

FOREST FIRES

BY PATRICK MERRI

Published by The Child's World®
1980 Lookout Drive • Mankato, MN 56003-1705
800-599-READ • www.childsworld.com

ACKNOWLEDGMENTS
The Child's World®: Mary Berendes, Publishing Director
Olivia Gregory: Editing

PHOTO CREDITS
© Bbsimpson/Dreamstime.com: 18; Coisax/Dreamstime.
com: 5; Collective91/Dreamstime.com: 17; Duncan Noakes/
Dreamstime.com: cover, 1; Irene1601/Dreamstime.com:
9; Fttsftts/Dreamstime.com: 15; Groke/Dreamstime.com:
13; Ruslan Absurdov/Shutterstock.com: 7; Starletdarlene/
Dreamstime.com: 21; Tupungato/Dreamstime.com: 10

ISBN 9781631437663
LCCN 2014945415

Printed in the United States of America
Mankato, MN
November, 2014
PA02245

ABOUT THE AUTHOR

Patrick Merrick was born in California and spent much of his early life moving from town to town and from state to state. Patrick now lives in Minnesota with his wife and children. When not busy teaching school, writing, or parenting, Patrick enjoys the occasional nap.

Table of Contents

4   Forest Fire!

6   Anywhere, Anytime

8   Just One Spark

11   Destructive Fires

12   Fire Fighting

14   Helpful Fires

19   Prevention

22   Glossary

23   To Find Out More

24   Index

Forest Fire!

It is very dry in the forest. It hasn't rained in weeks, and the woods are getting drier every day. But soon rumbling storm clouds hang in the sky. A hot wind blows, and lightning flashes. Black smoke curls up from the dry forest grass. Then hot, orange flames spread from the grass to the trees. It's a forest fire!

Fire is used by everyone. We cook with it. We heat our homes with it. We even light fireworks with it! Even though fire is very useful, it can also destroy things. Forest fires are one type of fire that can be very harmful. That's because forest fires can spread quickly and burn many **acres**, or areas of land, at one time.

This forest fire is roaring through a forest in Portugal.

Anywhere, Anytime

Three things are needed for a fire: fuel, air, and a heat source. Firefighters call this the "fire triangle."

Forest fires can happen anywhere there are trees and grasses. And when the weather has been very dry, forest fires can happen a lot! Without rain, the trees and grasses that grow in a forest get very dry. With just one spark a forest fire can begin. And with the help of a hot, dry wind, a forest fire can spread quickly to other parts of the forest.

Dry pine needles, leaves, twigs, and other things are fueling this forest fire.

Just One Spark

Eight out of every ten forest fires are caused by people.

Forest fires and wildfires can move up to 14 miles (23 km) per hour.

Starting a fire on purpose is called "arson."

All a forest fire needs to start is a spark. Usually, the spark comes from lightning during a storm. Sometimes, though, a forest fire will start in other ways. A volcano can start forest fires with the hot, liquid rock, called **lava**, that flows from the volcano's peak. Sparks that come from falling stones or rubbing branches can also start forest fires. But people can start forest fires, too.

People can start forest fires in many ways. They forget to watch their campfires and trash fires while they are staying in the forest. Sometimes people leave the forest without making sure that their campfire is out all the way. And other people throw their cigarettes into the dry grass. By being careless, people are now the biggest cause of forest fires.

Windy days and nights are some of the most dangerous times to build campfires.

9

Destructive Fires

Forest fires are very dangerous. Many birds and other forest animals die because of forest fires. Even fish can die in forest fires because the water in which they live becomes too hot! Forest fires can also spread to places where people live. When this happens, the fires burn houses, buildings, and trees in people's yards.

Even after a forest fire has been put out, it can still destroy things. Forest fires make the ground and air in a forest very hot. This heat can destroy the soil that keeps trees and ground together. If it rains after a forest fire, many times the burned ground washes away in huge mudslides. These mudslides can destroy the forest even more by blocking rivers and streams.

Downed power lines sometimes start forest fires.

Firefighters often name forest fires after a nearby meadow, creek, or town.

A large fire can create winds of over 100 miles (161 km) per hour!

This forest in Spain was destroyed by a fire. You can see that the ground is covered in ash.

Fire Fighting

Large animals are often able to escape a forest fire.

Some fires produce small tornadoes of fire called "fire whirls."

Fire lines are sometimes called "firebreaks."

Forest rangers watch for fires from high lookout towers. If they see any smoke, they call firefighters right away. Firefighters use water from nearby rivers or lakes to help put out the fire. If there isn't any water nearby, they bring in water using large tanker trucks, airplanes, or helicopters.

Sometimes it takes more than water to put out a forest fire. By using shovels and rakes, firefighters can beat down the flames before they spread. Sometimes, they build **fire lines** to stop the fire from spreading. They do this by clearing the land around the fire. The fire goes out without things to burn.

This helicopter is dropping water on a forest fire that has gotten too close to a city.

Helpful Fires

Pine trees need forest fires to help their seeds. Pinecones open up with a fire's heat. The seeds inside can then grow in the months after the fire has passed.

Forest fires get rid of plants that have diseases, allowing the new growth to start fresh and healthy.

Fires are helpful in another way: they kill large numbers of insects that can be pests to plants and animals.

For many years, people thought that all forest fires were bad. Today, scientists know that fires are actually good for forests. Without fires, some forest trees grow too big and block the sun. Without the sun, small forest plants and young trees can't grow. And without the small plants, there is nothing for many forest animals to eat.

This forest in Alaska is slowly growing back after a fire years before.

A "crown fire" is a fire that spreads across the treetops.

A fire in 1988 destroyed over one million acres (almost 405,000 hectares) of Yellowstone National Park.

Fighting forest fires is a very dangerous job. In 2013, 19 firefighters died trying to control a fire in Arizona.

Fires are so important to forests that some firefighters are trained to start them on purpose! These **burn crews** study and understand the fires they start. They watch their fires carefully and only burn small areas so that new trees can grow. Burn crews also watch forest fires started by lightning and let them burn as long as they stay under control.

Here you can see a member of a burn crew as he starts a grass fire.

Prevention

While some fires help forests, the ones made by careless people can destroy them. For that reason, it is very important to learn how to prevent forest fires. Being careful in the forest and not playing with matches are two good ways of preventing forest fires. If you are camping, let someone who knows about fire be in charge of the campfire.

Never leave a campfire unattended.

If you do not have any water to put out a campfire, use dirt and sand.

This sign in Georgia's Chattahoochee National Forest reminds people to be careful not to start fires.

A forest fire will always spread in the direction in which it can get the most from the "fire triangle."

When it is time to go home, make sure that your campfire is out all the way. You can do this by pouring water over the fire and then putting dirt on any glowing pieces of wood. Above all, always listen to the warnings of the forest rangers. They understand forest fires and how dangerous they can be. If everyone is careful in nature, there will be more forests for people to enjoy.

Some park rangers, like this one in Yosemite National Park, ride on horseback.

Glossary

acres (AY-kurz)

Acres are measurements of land. One acre equals 0.4 hectares. Forest fires can burn many acres of land at one time.

burn crew (BURN KROO)

A burn crew is a group of special firefighters that start fires on purpose. These fires help control the forests.

fire line (FIRE LINE)

A fire line is an area around a fire that is cleared. A forest fire goes out without things to burn.

lava (LAH-vuh)

Lava is hot, melted rock that comes from the inside of volcanoes. If lava flows into a forest, fires can start.

To Find Out More

In the Library

Beil, Karen Magnuson. *Fire in Their Eyes: Wildfires and the People Who Fight Them*. San Diego, CA: Harcourt Brace, 1999.

Peluso, Beth A. *The Charcoal Forest: How Fire Helps Animals & Plants*. Missoula, MT: Mountain Press, 2007.

Simon, Seymour. *Wildfires*. New York: HarperCollins, 1996.

Trammel, Howard K. *Wildfires*. New York: Children's Press, 2009.

On the Web

Visit our Web site for links about forest fires:
www.childsworld.com/links

Note to Parents, Teachers, and Librarians: We routinely check our Web links to make sure they're safe, active sites—so encourage your readers to check them out!

Index

acres, 4
Alaska, 14
Arizona, 16
arson, 8

burn crews, 16

campfires, 8, 19, 20
causes, 6, 8
Chattahoochee National
    Forest, 19
crown fire, 16

damage, 11

effects on weather, 4

fighting fires, 12, 16
fire lines, 12
fire triangle, 6, 20
fire whirls, 12
firebreaks, 12
forest rangers, 12, 20

Georgia, 19

importance of, 14

lava, 8
lightning, 4, 8, 16
lookout towers, 12

mudslides, 11

naming, 11

Portugal, 4
preventing, 19, 20

Spain, 11

United States, 4

winds, 4, 6, 11

Yellowstone National Park, 16
Yosemite National Park, 20